Please thank you but why

poems by

Lysbeth Em Benkert

Finishing Line Press
Georgetown, Kentucky

Please thank you but why

ACKNOWLEDGMENTS

Scurfpea Press Anthology (2018)—a ghost of my former self; Re-creations (re-
titled Ephemera); Literally (retitled, Morning Prayers),
Persephone's table, *Bombay Gin 46 Visionary Hauntology* (2020)
Thinking like a glass cat, *Pasque Petals* (2018)

Publisher: Leah Huete de Maines
Editor: Christen Kincaid
Cover Art and Design: Sara Christiansen-Blair
Author Photo: Jennifer Vaughn

Order online: www.finishinglinepress.com
also available on amazon.com

Author inquiries and mail orders:
Finishing Line Press
PO Box 1626
Georgetown, Kentucky 40324
USA

Contents

Agathism

sounds like agony,
like we have to suffer for it,
like nothing is free,
like everything has a price,
like we're always on a fence line,
like agnostic,
like we believe but don't believe we deserve it,
like agape with wonder and terror,
like agapé—love so hard it hurts,
like optimism is a risk,

like I'm afraid to hope but still I can't help myself.

Dear Persephone

"Now Proserpina, as a Deity, of equal merit, in two kingdoms reigns:—for six months with her mother, Demeter, she abides,and six months with her husband, below."
—Ovid's *Metamorphoses*

You love pomegranates.
Such a baffling fruit—
a fistful of garnets
and memories of sunshine.

I prefer pedestrian indulgences.
Chambersburg peaches slurpy, sweet, soft,
dripping down my chin,
my arm
my shirt,

an excess.

Is that too easy?
should pleasure come in little bits after a great deal of work,
be exotic and mysterious,
be worthy of dreams,
savoring of springtime and death.

Perhaps.

It's true,
my peaches are long ago
sliced,
frozen,
sealed in jars,
savored,
and gone.

Now I eat apples
and drink strong, dark coffee.

It seems more important to just pay attention,
not feel the long, slow slide of warm syrup on my skin.

Perhaps.

If you can explain these things to me
some time,

I promise to pay attention.

Not the answer you're looking for

"Eg havi lúkað Treytin tín. Eg havi hildið Trú fyri vist"
("I have solved your problem well. I have kept my word to you.")
—*Loki to his petitioner in the Loka Tattur**

The desert is saturated
with unrealized potential,
alive and burning.
No. I won't offer an example.
Adapt.
Hold your breath.
It's an endurance test,
and sometimes it sums zero.

No. I won't offer an example.
Adapt.
Push your fingers into your chest,
and pull out a lump of flesh.
It's best if you drop that
at the front desk.

Hold your breath—
it's an endurance test.
Once disburdened
you are both more and less.

Sometimes it sums zero.
The desert is saturated with unrealized potential.
The deluge scours your sacrifice from the altar.
It's mine now.

Alive and burning,
it's an endurance test.
No, I won't offer an example.
Adapt, and hold your breath.

* Trans. Alexa Duir, Math Jones, and Denise Vast. 2021 Nov. https://www.mimisbrunnr.info/lokka-tattur-vast-et-al-2021.

Letters from Liminal Spaces

I don't even know where to send this.

You were always on a quest—
never all the way here.
And then gone altogether.

Always looking for something.

You were so alive you couldn't contain yourself—
opening your veins occasionally
to let some of you leak out.

Leechcraft with a kitchen knife.

You were a ball of fire.
You were a smile
as bright as the shades flapping open at noon.

You were eyes as dark as the arctic sea—
like whirlpools,
like black holes,
sucking us in,
then closing us out.

I don't even know where to send this.

You were always on a quest,
but never running toward something.

Always away.

You were always running away.

What Dreams May Come

There's an absence
in the aching not-truth of this life
that becomes a quest—

searching for the lightning source
of an after image,
searching for a voiceless whispering,

until the constant movement
becomes a fruitless tramping
through dreamscape,

under a sickly amber sky,
filled with a rumbling
but no storm.

It is a not-death made possible
because some pattern spelled out "*invisible*"
after the blood whorled through shimmering water,

made possible by trading on a black market
of secrets.
It's what had to be done.

When you wake, those walking shadows
coalesce into myths solid as the multiverse itself.
You grin a wolfish smile

and reach for the glimmering threads beneath all there is,
piece together the patchwork of this world,
prepare to draw down the lightning,

to fill that empty space within,
knowing, when it kills you,
you will feel everything.

Persephone's table

Hades, who rulest the all-holding realm,
and thou, Persephone, I pray, boldly to speak of powers
hidden away and buried beneath the earth.
    —*Seneca, Hercules Furens*

Here is what I think—

maybe
it's a murmuration of black birds sinuous against the sunset,
searching for the lost tribes of my ancestors—
all those Jeans.

maybe
it's drinking red pop on the front porch,
sweating in the hazy sunshine
while the maple leaves dance to the shouting blue jays in their branches.

maybe
it's what happens when Elizabeth Tudor finally snaps at Sir Walter,
"don't be a dick,"
and he lets the black moth fly into the darkness.

maybe
it's when my sinister hand is no longer smudged with ink,
when lethargy surprises caffeine into a well-deserved nap,
when I stop asking, "what's in this box?"

maybe
it's when the owl swoops low across the sidewalk at twilight—
startling, enormous—and disappears
in precisely a way that should be impossible—

            dizzying, graceful, and utterly silent.

Rebirth

Over the sea from the north sails a ship with the people of Hel,
at the helm stands Loki.
        —*Voluspo, The Poetic Edda*

You are awake now.
Green gems blink out of the mist,
a sculpted mouth curving like a horizon—
a promise.

You live a half life
in two worlds
eating their scraps
no place at the table.

Move forward through the ash,
black and gritty,
thoughts caught between the rock in your fist
and a paradox.

Your heart burns—
a volcanic mass,
a furnace forging dreams
out of ravens' blood.

Arm yourself with demons.
They expect
nothing better
from a Monster like you.

Mundificative

sounds like the dirt before soap,
like the mineral plaster sucking out the toxins,
like the catalyst that sparks the reaction but fails to be consumed,
like you have to be foul before cleansed,
lost before found,
fucked up in order to get your second chance because repenting after
sliding through on gray mediocrity isn't enough for redemption,

and doesn't that smell like damnation heralded by Mary's least
memorable psalm.

Which is the littlest god?

There are, actually, long stretches of time where everything seems fine, really. There are conversations. He says he loves you. And it doesn't really matter at all that he doesn't hold your hand, or touch your hair. Because there are no landmines beneath the carpet.

But then someone doesn't show up for their shift,
leaves a big job that has to be covered,
right when some other project is due.
And he isn't angry at you.
But it doesn't feel that way.
He isn't yelling at you.
But that's not how your body hears the words.
He says it's not about you.
But the words come with exclamation points.

And your body
doesn't know
the difference.

He curses an appliance. You feel it in your spine.
He yells at the sharp corner on the basement ceiling,
you feel it across your back.
You curl up in on yourself,
waiting for it to blow over.
Waiting for him to leave the room.
Waiting until he goes to bed.
Waiting.

Still harping on daughters

Ophelia
is a non-action hero—
an un-hero,
anti-heroine,
whatever.

She saves herself.
Sometimes.

Her soliloquys are melodies
hummed tunelessly
as she tiptoes through
the broken promises
of her father's living room.

Her epiphany
hangs on a coat hook
behind the door
under the rain coat,
beside the forgotten pledge
of a soft black scarf.

When she burnishes her bodkin
she is granted three gifts

      her first gift is joy—
      a quiver in her heart
      fed by paper sonnets,
      little fluttering emissaries
      of music vows

      her second is duty—
      a silent ornament,
      legal tenderness,
      currency with which to buy
      her father's ambition

      her third is freedom
      purchased with spare change,
      a few words,
      and a tall glass of water,

while her garments,
heavy with their drink,
pull her under.

With that last breath,
does she pray to Persephone
to mingle darkness
with blossoms—
rosemary,
pansies,
rue?

or does she pray to the nightingale
to fill her lungs
with broken songs—
ballads warbled
without tongue to give them shape?

Either way,
the silence is the only promise she gets to keep.

Thinking like a glass cat

"A Glass Cat! . . . She has a pretty blood-red heart,
but it is made of stone—a ruby I think—and so is rather hard and unfeeling."
　　—L. Frank Baum, *The Patchwork Girl of Oz*

No more warm prayers in triplicate.
I want to box mine off in fours—
I'll build a sharp theosophy,
by sweeping cobwebs.

Biology rejects the clean
of sharper angles, fractals bloom
alongside curves. They shift. They slide.
Inchoate.

Volcanos belch forth quatrains. Birth
clean symmetry in silicate
form crystal shapes, tetrahedron
lattices,

corners, edges—frozen souls,
fixed. Facets order disorder—
quartz, garnet, topaz, rubies.
Solid hearts that need not beat.

Symbol-making animals

Physics orders the universe—
dictates distance between
molecules, attraction between
atoms, it shapes matter into
crystalline forms and fractals, rules
even the amorphous gathering
of insects, the ephemeral
glittering of their wings.

A smear of light refracts across
the darkening horizon,
foreshadowing the rising moon
only by force of will,
only because we ask why,
only because we insist
that indifferent photons
bent blood red by dust
signify
something.

But the half-life of perfume
is only the slow dispersal of volatile compounds.
It's loss that turns us into liars.

The trap of hope is an act of interpretation—
a grasping after immortality in the glass of memory,
a sin against the predestination of physical entropy
through the chaos of choice,

as though speaking meaning will make it so.

Cognitive Dissonance

Dear Mnemosyne,
how you must resent us,
our casual re-writing of narrative,
how we selectively edit our past
seeing only what we want,
transforming
by
re-naming.

You see everything—
the pain of childbirth,
the ecstasy of death.
Loci anchor your memories
while ours float away from their moorings.

Language traps you,
encoding history in your flesh.
It is the breath you inhale,
the blood filling your dreams,
the tears dripping from your chin,
the sweat pooling between your breasts.

Forgive us—
the best we can do is live
in little pockets of joy
where we find them,

the brief impression of our lives
like eating ice cream in the rain,
and the sweetness on our tongues
our only offering.

Please thank you but why

"Happy is he whom the Muses love: sweet flows speech from his mouth.
For though a man have sorrow and grief in his newly-troubled soul
and live in dread because his heart is distressed, yet, when a singer,
the servant of the Muses, chants the glorious deeds of men of old
and the blessed gods who inhabit Olympus, at once he forgets his heaviness and
remembers not his sorrows at all; but the gifts of the goddesses soon turn him
away from these."
　　　　　—Hesiod's *Theogony*

Nine girls would be a handful for any mother.
Mnemosyne does her best, but she cannot be all things
everywhere.
Their father has long since left and re-married;
their jealous step mother does not care for them,
so they keep their distance.
Dad's a little squicky, anyway.

Polyhymnia, muse of sacred poetry and grammar, is the eldest,
the enforcer of please and thank you,
　　　　of fold-your-hands, and bow-your-head,
　　　　of don't-say-ain't,
　　　　of there-is and there-are.
She is admired and avoided.

Poly picks at her sister Erato, a lover,
"muse of errors, not eros," Poly snaps.
　　　　"Your shirt is too tight,
　　　　your skirt too short.
　　　　You stayed out too late.
　　　　It's dangerous. You're dangerous. We're in danger."
Erato rolls her eyes,
sneaks out the second-story window after dark.

Poly's favorite is Terpsichore, the dancer.
She is the baby.
Her easy smile lures her eldest sister out of her foul mood,
　　　　she wears gauzy blouses,
　　　　forgets her doctor's appointments,
　　　　remembers everyone's birthdays.
She soothes and smiles and deflects Poly's fury,
until her sister forgets her anger,
forgets why the sweaty glass on the coffee table was such an offense.

Thalia, too, feels the weight of Poly's rules,
fights back with biting satire.
Her sharp smile is set off by
                black hair,
                black nail polish,
                black dresses,
                black boots,
                black lipstick,
and she carries her razor-wit in a sheath on her hip.
Poly hears her lectures played back to her in dramas
that leave her sisters in stitches, their sides aching,
leave Poly lying in the dark, tears drying in her hair.

Melpomene is Thalia's twin,
her photonegative—
a bright smile dressed in a riot of colors—
                dizzy red jacket,
                flower t-shirt,
                lime green skinny jeans.
She laughs easily at her sister's bitter jokes.
When Thalia loses her voice,
Mel spins bloody tales of poetic justice.

Clio, Calliope, and Urania—history, epic, and astronomy—
have marathon study sessions in the library.

Euterpe is a loner, a daydreamer,
singing snatches of lyrics to herself.
                She wears purple,
                dyes her hair to match her shining dark nails.
She sits on the roof under the shade of a big silver maple
just listening,
comes in only when Poly begs,
                "Play me a song, Eu.
                Sing to me;
                I can't sleep."

Poly's other prayers clog the bathroom sink,
caught in the hair she trimmed from her bangs
when she locked the door because

Ijustwanttobeleftaloneplease,
and who would she pray to anyway?
Best turn off the faucet,
clean her sacrifice from the scissors,
and consign her gifts to silence.

Atlas

In the cold Easter Sunday rain,
tiny bright daffodils nod,
and carry the weight of the cathedral on their roots.

Peregrination

sounds like flying,
spiraling on updrafts in the jet stream toward no place in particular
when you ought to be moving forward, making progress, going
on an expedition pilgrimage quest to find yourself whoever that
might be, feathers ruffled with knowledge fresh killed and still
warm, not on some junket or jaunty ramble where you might as
well be on some noctambulation stumbling in the dark knocking
about through the waste bins populating your dreams which are
not visions prophecies revelations brought by terrifying angels,
but only a replay of what kept you grounded during office hours
instead of keening high in the air like the wild thing you long to be.

Measuring in candle feet

Persephone is a gracious hostess,
maiden of spring, of transitions,
waiting by the threshold,
hair lit by the watery light that filters
through the leaded transept.
She throws back the dead bolt
pulls open the great oaken door
and raises an eyebrow—
a query,
in or out, girl?

I cannot see past the front porch,
only glimpse
hazy mythological possibilities,
a masque dancing
its algebraic magnificence—
poetry that refuses Charity
and offers none.

The entryway creaks under the weight of tradition,
tattered cobwebs drift,
the house breathes
catches at my clothing
ghosts across my cheek.
Glistering dust traps sunlight
angling through the gaps in the curtains,
and Persephone still waits,
tells stories
of the hope of death,
the terror of birth.
She never promises.
Never once does she say,
I promise.

On which step shall I lower my weight
and rest?
Toward what occasion shall I walk?
To what ephemera,
under what canopy
shall I raise my glass?

In or out, girl?
I can't hold this door open forever.

Morning prayers

If words could kill
we would always
be picking up pieces of ourselves—
a finger over there
an eyeball from under the couch.

Every morning
I glue myself together with sighs
I sit up
—one deep breath—
walk down the hall
—another—
dress and pull on my boots
—inhale again—
then slowly fall apart

a pile of words
a poem
a gift as brief as a sigh
a bouquet of heartsease
a fistful of bleeding hearts

Sybil, listening

It comes out in tears,
drip after drop of salt and brine.

Oceans of dissolved facts lost in Kleenexes—
vast ponds of knowledge (complete with ducks),
reservoirs of wisdom chlorinated and drunk,
waterfalls pounding exhausted salmon,
splooshes of intellect alongside the road,
arbitrary facts bombarding umbrellas from above

(I heard you say that god's pissing on us—
he's pissing on all of us).

Drops of wasted wisdom from above—
falling down,
flowing over,
sinking in,
drying up,
blowing away,
until they are gathered together
into boxes of insta-fax
to which
one must
simply
add
water
and
drink.

Waiting at the speed of light

Fleeing from him, they seemed to rise on wings,
and it was true, for they had changed to birds.
Then Philomela, flitting to the woods, found refuge in the leaves.
    —*Ovid's Metamorphoses*

She paused at an abyss she believed impossible to travel,
imagined what lay at the bottom—

crushed tin cans,
empty diaries with stubby pencils,
worn out shoes with broken laces,
sea glass ground smooth as pebbles.

imagined the metamorphoses—

larvae to mayflies,
eggs to hummingbirds,
atoms to energy,
breath to song.

Keep Going

From the Great Above Inanna opened her ear to the Great Below.
My Lady abandoned heaven and earth to descend into the underworld.
Inanna abandoned heaven and earth to descend into the underworld.
        —from The Descent of Inanna

The road to hell is paved with grudging respect,
full of primrose motivations,
lined in reckless disquiet.

I try to remember what I came for,
what made it worth the trip.

This pilgrimage demands every precious thing tethering me to life,
takes the riches I relinquish as tribute,
takes the devotion from my eyes,
takes the strength with which I was clothed,
until I arrive in rags.

To pay for my transgressions
my limbs remain my only tender,
so Sacrifice lifts my torso up
and Duty hooks my corpse to the wall.

Who now to plead my case?
What friend's bloody, blind hands will lift my corpse,
return me to my feet,
bathe me, and tell me that I have given enough?

Only when her left hand bargains with the darkness
can my right pull the barb from my chest,
can I claw my way back,
the way curvaceous, sharp-cornered,
crossed with blind alleyways and one-way streets.

She reminds me to find the x on my map;
now is a bad time to get lost.

She reminds me of my bargain,
the debt of tears I've paid, that I still owe.

We try to forget the hook tethering my flesh to loss,
forget the darkness that drove me underground,
and step back into the light.

Transmogrification

sounds like mongrel,
like dogs who've traveled all over and now just want to have a good
lie down on a soft carpet, but when they close their eyes, they
dream of chasing strange mutant squirrels and their feet twitch
while they swim across bottomless rivers and their sleepy lungs
huff at coyotes across highways built from smells blown by autumn
breezes, so when they open their eyes, they still love you but they'll
never look at you quite the same again.

Burning Love

Elvis ruminates from a small
ranch house in the suburbs.

They say I look like a preacher,
that I should give the readings on Sunday.

Maybe I will.
Maybe I'll go online and get a license.

Maybe I'll stand up at that pulpit
on Sunday and preach the Good Word,

as soon as I remember which word
and whether I have to pick just one.

Do I need a word of sesquipedalian proportions,
large enough to contain swiveling hips,
rhinestone jackets,
shifting petticoats,
and vacant shag carpet living rooms?

or will a small word do,
one whose meaning shifts
between a curse and a blessing,
between agony and euphoria—
sweat slick and breathless?

I had a garage sale and cleaned house,
threw open the blinds and polished my Gibson;
I'm halfway through this love song
and about ready to start the bridge.

Let me channel that brightness
and serve as a vessel for grace.

A ghost of my former self

This is my ode to
useless things—
immortal dust bunnies,
cobwebs
too high
to reach,
skeletal leaves caught
in puddles,
nana's lipstick,
grandma's powder.

I will sing for
forgotten things—
plastic forks with broken
tines,
tiny ends
of pink erasers,
rolling screws in cluttered
junk drawers,
man-
gled springs from
broken pens.

I will be the goddess of
what's
post-pragmatic—
keys to
diaries long disposed of,
broken necklace
links,
watches who've
untimely met their makers,
a twist-
ed clasp,
a
dressless sash.

In my wake

Don't lie to me,
lie about me,
grab someone's lapels
—anyone's—
and tell extravagant prevarications—
glorious lies.

Say I fought elves in the Pyrenees,
that I sang ballads with Welsh bards
about ocean eyes and kitten soft hair,
sailed in the tear-wet moonlight
and spoke with mermen in three languages,

say I recited heroic couplets
with a be-sotted Shakespeare
and his blushing lover, Keats,

or that I played strip poker with Hecate
and made love
under a blood moon in a field
purged with the plasma heat of our kisses.

Promise
that you will not tell the truth.

Promise
to drink deep.

Promise
that you'll lie.

Future Perfect

In the cottage
near the pond
there's a ribbon
fallen

     on
     the
     tiles,
there's a shadow across white sheets,
bruises left by a storm,
and a memory of tanned skin.

Beneath the water,
     she holds.
     her breath.
     and listens.
     to the pulse.
     of blood.
     in her ears—
     weightless
     and unburdened
     by decisions,
     by fortune.

Back on the dock,
sunlight becomes solid,
     refracting
          off
             watery
                undulations,

and she could step out,
walk across that blinding brightness,
fish brushing against the soles of her feet,
her sighs darting away—
mayflies escaping a net.

Ephemera

A young woman looks out at me from sepia photographs—
        jaunty smile,
        bobbed hair,
        sparkling eyes—
        as much a myth to me as Pallas Athena.
        Her fashionable dresses and
        daring swimsuits
        look nothing like
        my grandmother
        bent double
        as her bones
        betrayed her.

Here is what I have left of her:
        a dozen mismatched champagne glasses that sing when I wash them,
        eggshell china soup cups,
        a tiny glass pitcher from the 1895 Worlds Fair,
        a leather-bound jewelry box with a spring-loaded clasp,
        a silver thimble,
        a salt cellar,
        a pile of costume jewelry I never wear,
        a half-dozen crystal liqueur glasses.

I never saw her use any of them.

Here is what I remember:
        the teeth she never wore,
        housedresses,
        crossword puzzles,
        endless cups of instant coffee,
        crinkly cigarette packets,
        quizzes in the kitchen over times tables,
        the whistle of her lungs as she walked up the stairs.

I never thought to question what wore her so thin:
        hands more bone than flesh,
        skin paper soft,
        heart an open book
        in a language I'll never know.

Medusa's children

Garter snakes hibernate in knots,
wintering wrapped about one another in dens,
in logs, under rocks,
tangled in piles
like discarded yarn,
a glossy tapestry snarled
by clumsy fat fingers,
something
un-made.

Warmth resurrects them,
an undifferentiated assemblage of snakeyness,
coiling around each other,
a mass of writhing pheromones.
A singularity—
potential energy
driven to multiply,
to be more,
to fill the world with their silky selves

before blossoms
come,
before heroes
wake,
before the heat
of the sun pulls them apart.

Shedding skin

you sang kumbaya
by a bonfire,
the big logs like a funeral pyre,

a way to make peace,
draped in a buffalo hide
while women told stories

—better than I'm telling this one now—
about a quest,
about a shot through the heart,

about the sacred, bloody work
of skinning the buffalo,
and tanning the hide,

about wrapping yourself
in its carcass
to keep warm.

If you had a little pouch
to put your stories in,
what would you collect?

a tuft of wiry white fur
caught in the green tundra—
snow in summer

the surprise at the resonant
thunk of a deerskin drum
after silence

the bright spark
that escapes the fire
into the darkness

the ash
left in the morning
on your fingertips

Agīfan: to give in return

Skin slides across skin—silk warmed by sunshine,
fragranced with the sweat of the ocean,
tasting of its salty tang,
and the sweet lemonade of your chapstick.

My friend Candace paints pictures of Chincoteague Island,
the joy of its wild horses chasing the diamond spray of the shore,
flank bumping against flank,
the wuff of breath ruffling a mane.
When I close my eyes,
their hoofbeats rain down on my dreams.

When I wake, I'll walk my dog and drink my tea
and read about a madman who blamed his addiction on temptation,
who sought to erase his sins by painting women in red.
I'll remember a man who claimed to sacrifice himself for me
by becoming a bystander in his own life.

The open wound of intimacy is a mouth
begging to be sewn shut, to be silenced,
just as it begs to be licked into, tasted,
sucked clean.

To find your wounds,
I will ride into your surf on the back of a palomino,
feel its muscles shift beneath my thighs.
You will take my fear into yourself

and hand it back to me on your lips.
When I breathe you in,
and fill my hungry lungs with your heat,
I will say I do not need you.
This will be a lie.

Cross that swan road when you come to it.
Its brine will speak to the salt water that pumps beneath our skin,
while the wind unbinds the scarf at your neck
and it floats free.

Lysbeth Em Benkert grew up in southwestern Pennsylvania where she was blessed with parents who were addicted to paperbacks. She learned a love for words early, raiding her parents' bookshelves and writing reams of poetry.

After high school, Lysbeth attended the all-female Chatham College before moving west to complete graduate degrees in English literature from Washington State University and eventually settle down in South Dakota to teach Shakespeare, Rhetorical Theory, and composition.

For some reason, though, creative writing dropped out of her life for many years. She did not take it up again until the mid-2000s, when she audited a creative writing class taught by her excellent and talented friend, Pen Pearson. Dr. Pearson offered the encouragement and constructive criticism that re-lit a desire to write. Not only that, but Dr. Pearson invited her to join the Women Poets Collective, founded by Christine Stewart-Nuñez, whose manuscript feedback and emotional support have been nothing short of transformational. Readers will, in fact, find several books written by WPC members in Finishing Line Press's catalog, including collections by Marcella Remond, Erika Saunders, Jeanne Emmons, and Lindy Obach. This community of writers helped usher into the world two chapbooks for Lysbeth. The first, *#girl stuff*, was published in 2018 by Dancing Girl Press. The second here, *Please thank you but why*, with Finishing Line Press.

www.ingramcontent.com/pod-product-compliance
Lightning Source LLC
Chambersburg PA
CBHW022045080426
42734CB00009B/1239